So You Think You're Ready?

So You Think You're Ready?

Demond A. Warren

authorHOUSE®

AuthorHouse™
1663 Liberty Drive
Bloomington, IN 47403
www.authorhouse.com
Phone: 1-800-839-8640

Published by AuthorHouse   03/15/12

ISBN: 978-1-4567-6739-6 (sc)
ISBN: 978-1-4567-6738-9 (e)

Contents

Introduction

My motive for writing this book is to restore the unity of the African-American family. There are values that we have strayed away from. So many African-Americans are not getting married because they fear that it will not work out. For those that do get married, fewer and fewer of those marriages are lasting. A great number of people get married with the mindset that if it doesn't work out they will just get a divorce. By having that mindset they are going into the marriage with an attitude of defeat. As I look around our nation, I see so many families breaking apart, thereby destroying future generations. We do what looks good, feels good, and whatever makes us happy as individuals. We are molding our next generation into self-centered out of control individuals going nowhere fast. The morals and values of our ancestors are almost extinct. The desire of my heart is for us to stop hurting and damaging one another. It's a catastrophic domino effect that seems like a never ending nightmare! We have to take the time to sit back and realize our selfishness only preps the next person for the same, or preps them to feel there's no way out of being nice and loving people and getting hurt, being someone's doormat! I wish to help restore the worth of our men and women; to revive the black community, putting things into proper perspective so that people who get married can STAY married, and for those that aren't married and are afraid of the marriage failing, to break free of that fear and fulfill their desire to be married. We don't have to accept a dysfunctional family as the norm! In order to establish and maintain a healthy family, our perspective on life has to be positive, with one main ingredient: love. It is the responsibility of each individual to do what's necessary to build a strong foundation that will solidify a successful relationship and/or marriage, even while you are still single.

It breaks my heart to see so many unhappy people. Whether they are unhappily married or unhappily single, many are miserable and have no clue as to why. In this book I will lay out some things very clearly, step by step, to help you understand why marriages fail, relationships crumb, and fear so gruesomely imprisons us.

PART I

To My Brothers

Chapter 1

The Young Bachelor

Young, fresh out of high school and headed to college, and ready to sow some wild royal oats! Every weekend you will go to the mall to get fresh, getting ready to hit up every 18 and older club you can. The thought of commitment is not even at the back edge of your brain. Your main goal is to have fun with your boys, getting with as many girls as you can. You know as long as you have money, getting girls is as easy as counting from 1-10. This is the life of a young male bachelor.

Going out with girls is fine. The not so fine thing is leading a young beautiful girl on to believe that she is the only one that you are dating, when the truth is you are dating 10. The number isn't important. The important thing is that you are making her think she is the only one. This builds your ego, making you think that you are God's gift to every woman. You think you are larger than life. You are setting yourself up for failure. Karma is patiently awaiting you.

There comes a time in every man's life that he meets an astonishingly beautiful young woman. She's intelligent, has class, and a body like she belongs on the front cover of a magazine. Her talk game is so smooth; she can get you to do literally anything for her . . . . anything. Then all of a sudden, she will hit you with the phrase, "I need some space." Then you start to think about all the times you though she might have been cheating. Now you're thinking she actually was cheating. You think back on the times she didn't answer the phone for a couple of hours and when she finally did she said she was sleep. You remember when you two first met she said she would never tolerate a man checking her cell phone because she will never check his. Now you realize she said that because she has something to hide. She could care less about what you are doing as long as you don't know what she's doing. You can remember a man that the two of you ran into at Wal-Mart. She introduced him as her cousin Chris, but you sensed that either they had a history of being kissing cousins or his real name was "Jody". Now you are hurting like a crack fiend needing a fix! You figure the only way to deal with the hurt and pain is to not deal with it at all. Not even realizing that you have reaped what you've sown, your plan now is to get back in the field, playing as many women as you can, never attaching yourself to any of them. This helps you to rebuild your confidence as a man, so you think. Before you met Ms. Mesmerize, you had so many women, that you had to dodge a couple of them by telling them you were a CPA that traveled out of state 5 days a week. After this very hurtful relationship, you are determined not to ever let that happen again at any cost.

This is very dangerous. You could possibly hurt the woman that will stalk you and cut your tires, which will only happen if she can't get her hands on you! I know you're thinking that only a woman with a rap sheet could do such a thing. This may be a surprise to you my brother, but it can happen with any woman. Her background could be squeaky clean. She could just be a woman scarred one time too many, tired of brothers treating her wrong when she has given her all, and now wants revenge. You may not realize it or you may not care, but you are hurting her, not knowing to what extent it could negatively affect her. Her self worth and esteem could be so damaged that she becomes bitter and develops the "protect myself" mentality, which can bring along anger, selfishness, intentional hurt to others, unforgiveness, and depression. She then will spread that negative energy to her friends and family, creating an influence for them to become the same way. But worst of all, she will impart that into her children. It snowballs from there. So instead of hurting innocent women and creating the possibility of getting yourself hurt, deal with the hurt from a relationship. The first step is to forgive the woman that hurt you, realizing that you are reaping what you've sown; hurt people hurt people. The next step is to keep busy, looking and moving forward to your bright future. Having a great support system is also very helpful. It's always great to have friends that understand and don't judge you. As much as you think you will groan with agony forever, in due time you will get over her and the pain will cease, maybe quicker than you think.

I have been hurt a time or two by women that I just knew I was going to marry. They obviously had other plans. I was seeing this woman that was 13 years older than me. She was from a small town in South Georgia. She was very beautiful. She had the complete package! Most importantly, she could cook! She wasn't throwing can goods in the pot brothers. She was from the old school. She cooked all of her vegetables fresh, made homemade cornbread, and at the drop of a dime would make my favorite dessert, banana pudding! I knew that I was too young for her, but she had everything I needed in a woman and I was more than willing to do all I could to show her that I was man enough for her. Sadly, without her even telling me and without seeing any evidence, I knew she had cheated on me. Of course when I confronted her she denied it. Eventually she admitted to it and I was extremely hurt. But, I was so in love, I forgave her and stayed with her. She used to call me crazy! I couldn't see myself with any other woman but her. But so much went on I finally manned up. After six months of perpetual drama, the relationship finally ended. It took months to get over her and the pain from all that she put me through. But once I was able to move on, I remained in humility. I didn't feel a need to take advantage of women that wanted to be loved just like me. It is important to treat people the way you want to be treated. If you feel that you are not ready for commitment, let every woman that you meet know that upfront. Don't lead her to think that there is even a chance she will have you to herself. If she wants to try hard to persuade you to commit to her and she doesn't succeed, it will be solely on her. She can only be mad at herself. This way you can still be free to have fun and see who you want to see, when you want to see them without hurting someone and getting yourself into major drama.

Chapter 2

Male Vs Man

It doesn't take any effort to be a male, but it takes a whole lot to be a man. A lot of males consider themselves to be men because they are hard working and financially stable. That is only a fragment. There are so many different aspects of being a mature man. A man takes care of ALL of his responsibilities, not just the ones that are most convenient for him. It takes a man to immediately admit when he is wrong. Ego trips are not a part of his character. He walks in humility at all times. He protects his family and does whatever he has to do to support them. He has a vision and a PLAN to carry out that vision. Instead of making excuses for why he can't accomplish his goals, he makes every effort to do what's necessary to achieve them. He is the initiator in his household. There are times when things don't go our way. It is fine to admit that you are perplexed, but you can't stay there. You have to encourage yourself and also have positive people in your life to encourage you to get back on your feet and keep running the race. If a man has children, no matter what the relationship is between him and the child/children's mother, he loves them as he loves himself and makes the necessary sacrifices for them. He is faithful, an affirmer, a teacher, a hero, which means he overcomes adversity, accomplishing that which he has set out to do, an earner, and he is responsible. He supports them financially, emotionally, and supports any of their positive activities. I can't understand for the life of me why brothers make children and don't take care of them. It really bothers me to see a single mother struggling to take care of her children and the father is still living, able, but not willing to help her take care of THEIR children. It is true that there are some women out there that are vindictive and will not allow the father to be a part of the child's life. However, if the mother wants you to take part in raising them, you should be more than happy and willing to do so. Brothers I have to say that if you are not taking care of your offspring, you are yet to be considered a man.

> When I was a child, I talked like a child, I thought like a child, and I reasoned like a child. When I became a man I put childish ways behind me. 1 Corinthians 13:11

One Woman Man

I know I'm going to get a lot of flack from you brothers for this, but I have to state the truth. It's fine to date more than one woman at a time. Dating is considered to be healthy for getting to know people and yourself. It's a great way to find out exactly what you feel you need in a woman, so that you can one day choose your jewel of a bride. However, it is not fine to date all these women and each of them thinks she's the only one! This is a great example of being on an ego trip. A man does not have to prove his manhood. You do not prove yourself to be a man by taking advantage of someone, getting gratification out of causing them pain and misery. Unfortunately, this is the behavior of the average male. Being a player is not cool. Trying to have your cake and eat it can get you into a world of trouble. Trust me on this fellas. Most of the time if you are open and honest with a woman, letting her know you are just dating right now and you want to take your time about choosing, she will want you that much more. You always want what you can't have. When you do make your selection, let the others know. Do not hold on to any of them, allowing them to think that they still have a chance with you. If you have a mature understanding with any of them that you will remain friends and only friends, there should be no interference with your monogamous relationship with the one you have chosen to be your significant other. If you see any signs of jealousy from any of these female friends, then it's time to say goodbye. She apparently emotionally can't handle just being your friend.

I hear so many women say that they can't find a good man. It's hard for us to find a good woman! Seriously, there are still a great number of phenomenal sisters out there that need a great man. I've asked several women why they don't have a man and they say because the brothers are not standing up being men. They are too busy being overgrown boys! Brothers, you have to understand that we are leaders. So many women today have become independent and feeling that they don't need a man. Even when they do get married, it's a common issue that the wife is so busy with her career that she's too tired or just has no interest for wifely duties. With online degree classes and lucrative career opportunities at their fingertips, they are taking advantage of every resource, preparing to be able to be self-sufficient. A vast number of women actually are fearful that they will have ex-husbands, so they feel the need to prepare themselves for singleness again on that great day of his exit. This explains why they are adamant about not letting anything get in the way of their careers and financial investments.

A woman should be able to be a woman. It's fine for a sister to have accomplished her goals and obtain wealth, but she should feel like she can come home and be that soft, sweet, and lovable confidant to her strong-minded, hard working, sensitive, and lovable man. She shouldn't have to feel like she has to take on your role. It was never intended by God for a woman to have the strength and role of a man. He compares her to a weaker vessel. This simply means she is the vessel that compliments the main one. He also refers to her as the help meet. God created woman to help him fulfill his purpose. God's plan for woman was to be man's partner in getting things done, which is why we need her for completion. It was never His intent for a woman to be completely in charge of the family. Now I am all for sharing certain responsibilities in the home, but just as a man has his role, a woman has her significant role as well.

Infidelity

Once a man has made the commitment to take a woman to be his wife, that should be the only woman he is sexually and intimately involved with. You have to understand that the institution of marriage is sacred in the eyes of God and the person you are married to. When I was married, I would see women everyday that were just as fine as my wife. Because I had undeniable love and respect for my wife and my marriage, I would not allow myself to go cheat on her. The temptation was murderous, but you have to have self-control to run from it.

I know some brothers that got married with the mindset that though they were getting married they were still going to get some on the side as much as they possibly could. This shows me that they are still boys not ready to love and surely not ready for marriage. Infidelity is a very dangerous game to play. So many people have been killed by their spouses because they were cheating. A mature man counts the costs and walks in self-control. He loves his wife as he loves himself. He treats her the way he wants to be treated, making any sacrifice that needs to be made for her.

Chapter 3

Fantasy Girl

It's a hot summer Friday afternoon and you just got off work. On your way home, you stop at the gas station to gas up for the weekend. As you're pulling up you see this obnoxiously beautiful young lady at the gas pump. She's wearing a pair of Derion skinny jeans that fit so tight it must have taken her an hour to get into them. She's standing about 5'2 with a waist size that looks to be about a 10. She has the perfect curves to perfectly fill in those jeans she's wearing. To top it all off, she has skin as smooth as a baby, long pretty hair that you can tell is not weave, and a smile that looks like a million bucks. As any man would, you approach her with the smoothest game you have ever come with, making sure you keep that smile on her face. She doesn't hesitate to give you her number. After a couple of days have passed, you call her, hoping that you don't say anything stupid that will turn her off. After a couple of very interesting mind stimulating conversations, you ask her out on a date. Already seeing that she can get anything she wants from you, she confidently says yes.

A couple of months go by and your emotions are really starting to get the best of you. You have been spending a great deal of time with her, taking her to places that you've never taken any other woman. She is everything that you have always dreamed of. Then suddenly, right at the height of it all, she stops answering your phone calls! When she does answer she is very short with you. She made sure to tell you that for the next couple of weeks she will be busy and she will not have as much time as usual to spend with you. The following Thursday you invite her over for dinner at your place on Friday night, just to take the edge off from such a busy week. You had planned to let her know how you feel about her and you were going to ask her if you could start seeing each other exclusively. Right in the middle of you asking her over for dinner she cuts you off and says that she thinks that the two of you should stop seeing each other. You're holding the phone feeling numb and confused. Everything was going perfect. She never complained about anything. You never even had one disagreement. You ask her why does she feel this way, but she doesn't want to give a reason. You hang up the phone, realizing you have just been played.

I wanted to paint this picture very vividly so that you would understand how quickly we go for the prettiest thing we see, later regretting that decision. As the old saying goes, everything that glitters isn't gold. There is a woman out there that is patiently waiting for the man of her destiny, and that man is you. She may not be shaped like the "Player Girl" from the gas station, but she is attractive and she walks in great character and, most importantly she will accept you for you. I truly believe that as long as you can look her in the face everyday, she treats you like the king you are and loves you inevitably, that is the one for you. Men are visual. However, you can't go by looks alone. You will regretfully miss out on a very great opportunity to be with a very great person.

A few years ago I met a very attractive young lady who was perfect for me. We had a fantastic relationship. We only had one disagreement when we first met. After that, everything was smooth sailing. As attractive as she was, she didn't quite fit the description of what I pictured my mate to be. Because we had several things in common, we spent a lot time together. That led to us getting close a lot faster than we intended. I was really feeling her at first, but after a few months pasted, that exciting feeling of being with someone that I clicked with so well with faded away. Oftentimes I would find myself flirting with other women that were what I considered to be dime pieces. I had two choices. I could either stay with her, knowing that she just wasn't doing it for me, which would mean eventually I would cheat on her, or I could opt out. She was really a great woman that did not deserve to be hurt. So, I decided to end it before it went any further.

Man do I regret that! Every woman that I came into contact with did me wrong! I didn't realize how shallow and vain I was being until all the "Video Vixens" I was chasing hurt me.

Being Realistic About Mrs. Right

Brothers, I believe that most of us have had the opportunity to be with an exceptionally great woman, but we were just too shallow to embrace her. In this day and time, it is very hard to come across a great woman of character. So many sisters now are either too busy with their careers to fully meet the needs of a man, in the clubs every weekend, wasting their precious time with a brother who is clearly not good for them, or too busy seeing other women! The day that you find that one that you can truly call your jewel, you better hold on to her forever. Knowing that you are a wonderful man, you deserve a wonderful queen to compliment you. This doesn't mean she has to look like Gabrielle Union. A man's queen has his back no matter what happens in the test of times. So many women today are quick to walk out on men the minute they see the least of adversities. The woman of your destiny should be humble and submissive, yet willing and able to speak he mind and stand her ground when truly necessary, confident and secure, a team player, patient, forgiving, and most of all, loves you for you unconditionally. When you meet this keeper, be faithful to her. Treat her as the queen that she is. If you don't, you may find another one, but you could possibly spend the rest of your life finding her. Reluctantly you will find yourself going on so many dates with women that are a total waste of your time. You may even run across one that you fall in love with and take her to the altar but she tramples over your heart. Always keep in mind that the woman of your destiny will be on one accord with you. She will be the only one, other than God, that can be your fortress.

Compatibility

Some time ago I was dating this very attractive young lady. She was a very faithful God-fearing woman. I can truly say she is a jewel.

We were friends for a while and we enjoyed the company of one another. We had certain things in common that helped to build a very strong bond. As close as we were, she still had personality traits that clashed with mine. It was cool being her friend, but I couldn't see myself spending the rest of my life with her, as her being my wife. But I kept thinking about the fact that she was such a great woman. To add to it, she really wanted to be with me. So, after nine months of being friends, I decided to go ahead and go for it. I knew I could trust her and she was madly in love with me. Unfortunately, our relationship came to a halt within a matter of a few weeks. While we were together I would always complain about certain things that I didn't understand about her. She said she wasn't going to put up with that and she broke it off with me. I couldn't blame her. Who wants to be with someone that is always complaining about them? I was either going to accept her for who she was or not be with her at all. For a couple of months we had no type of contact with each other. A few months later we tried it again. But after a couple of weeks I realized that we were meant to only be friends. Eventually she moved on and she is now happily married to someone that truly compliments her. It's very difficult sometimes finding that perfect fit.

A woman could have so many things going for herself, but you just can't seem to spark a flame. You have to be able to carefully discern if a person should just be your friend. However, in some cases it is true that good friends make for great lovers because you've already formed a bond. Every relationship has a purpose. A relationship is the sharing of time, information, and possibly emotions, and physical contact with another person. Some people you meet are meant to be business acquaintances, some mentors, some friends, and some for a season experience involving one or several learning lessons on your journey of life. There is only one person that God has prepared to be your spousal mate.

A very dear friend of mine has been married to his wife for 18 years. He told me that now that their children are all grown, he is leaving her. I was floored when he told me that. I couldn't believe that after 18 years of marriage a man could just leave his wife as if they have nothing. He said that he and his wife both agreed that they were never compatible. For the longest time they tried to fit together, but the chemistry just wasn't there. The person you are destined to be with will fit with you perfectly. It doesn't mean that you both are perfect. Subsequently, it does mean that you are compatible enough that you both desire each other, keeping the focus on the most important elements of your relationship, no matter what you come up against. There may be moments that you feel that you don't love that person emotionally, but with the development of Godly unconditional love, you work through those tough times. Lots of people spend years upon years with a person they were not destined to be married to. Being a great friend doesn't constitute one being a great spouse for you. It is great to be friends first before you enter into a monogamous commitment. Just make sure the chemistry is there. If you are genuinely passionate about each other and you walk in unconditional love with one another, you will make it to that altar.

The moral of the story is do not waste time trying to make something be that shouldn't be. Don't try to mold a woman into who you want her to be. Her personality makes her the person that she is. Find someone that you can enjoy on that level of commitment and embrace her, making her feel she can be herself at all times around you. That's a part of making a woman feel secure that she can trust you. If you really appreciate who she is and constantly compliment her, she will have no doubt in her mind that she can trust you. She will return that love to you one hundred times over. It's in her nature!

Chapter 4

How To Love Her

Overcoming Past Hurts

In order to give a woman the love that she needs, you have to be healed from any hurt and disappointments from your past so that you are open to love and be loved. This is the very thing that causes most men to be players and lead women on. If they've once put their heart on the line for someone and things didn't work out, then the usual response is vindication, making sure that it never happens again. This is just a way of saying, "I am insecure and afraid you will hurt me just like the other woman did." If you never deal with the hurt and heal from that hurt from your previous unproductive relationship you will continue the vicious cycle of hurting innocent women. In order to overcome pain from someone mistreating you in a relationship, you must take time to yourself, revitalizing your self-confidence and self worth. It can happen to anyone. We are human with human emotions that can be torn down.

For a lot of us even when we feel as though we've healed, we have a tendency to put up a wall that won't allow a person to fully love us neither does it allow us to love them back. This clearly says you have not healed nor forgiven the person or people who have wronged you. In order to trust anyone after being scarred, you must forgive your offenders. In fact, I believe that the very essence of your healing is in your forgiveness. Once you have done so, you will be open to love again. You will then be able to recognize the woman of your destiny.

Maybe you haven't been hurt by a woman. Maybe you are clueless as to how to be a man because you didn't have a father to show you the example. Therefore you have run from the responsibility of taking care of your child(ren). Maybe you have no idea how to commit to a woman, have problems communicating, abusive, or lacking good work ethic. Your only male influences were right there in your hood, which were drug dealers, pimps, and hustlers. Your first example of work ethic was standing on the corner all night selling an illegal product that was killing people of your own kind, day in and day out, but the financial outcome and the swiftness thereof was so attractive that it lured you into the game. Maybe your father was in your life but he did all the wrong things, so you followed his lead. You did not choose to be in that situation. You were born into it. But there is a man who is the SUPREME leader, never slacking in His role as a model of integrity, righteousness, and above all, love. Through all of the fellowship of brotherhood from the hood, you, unknowingly because all of the brush you looked up to told you that you had to defend for yourself, provide for yourself, and trust no one, needed to be loved. Mama loves you undeniably, but the leadership and untainted masculine influence you needed was not there. God loves you and has given you purpose. Your purpose does not involve mistreating women, deceiving people, and neglecting children. Allow Him to show you, through His word and divine instruction, how to think, thereby changing your ways, and ultimately your destiny. The truth of the matter is, hurt people hurt people. When you enter into a relationship or marriage broken, it's not that the relationship can't work, but the things that will come out of you could damage the person you are with. Relationships already require a lot of work, daily crucifying your flesh for the happiness and peace of your mate. Peace in your home doesn't come by continuous friction. It is better to have a stable, healed and peaceful heart and mind that to be bottled up with unanswered questions and unhealed wounds from your past. Everyone has something that they have experienced that affected them in a negative way. We have to make an executive decision that we are greater than our tragedies. It is from our tragedies that we are made strong. No great body builder gained maximum strength and massive muscular structure by lifting the same weight size he began with! Consciously read your bible daily for comfort, empowerment, and instruction. All that you need to break free and truly enjoy abundant life is in there. God's ways are the best ways to walk in valor. Change your life, change your family legacy!

The Meaning Of Unconditional Love

We often hear people say they are in love, but the minute that person they're in love with does something that disappoints them, they are ready to give up and leave. The term 'in love' is an expression of ones' emotional state at its' highest level. This type of love in its' Greek meaning is *eros, of* which the term erotica is derived from. It is described as passionate love with sensual desire and longing. You can be in love with someone and not love them unconditionally. You can simply be turned on emotionally by something they are doing to you or for you that gives that overwhelming emotional feeling, or just simply adore them for the very person that they are. Just as easily, that same person can do something you view as being inappropriate and those emotions will dissipate, causing you to feel emotionally down. Maybe even upset to the point of anger. Ironically that emotional high can flare up or melt down a million times over.

Unconditional love in its' greek meaning is *agapeo* or *agape*. When you love someone with gape love, they haven't done anything to earn it. You can be in love at first sight and/or with more than one person at a time, but you can only be faithfully and intimately committed to one of them, which is monogamy. You may be asking, "How can I love and be in love with more than one person at a time?" As I previously stated, being in love is just an emotional high. Several people at a time can make you feel this way. Agape love, however, is an inevitable trait from God that we all inherited from Him. We just have to operate in it! For most of us, we operate in that love when it is most convenient for us. In truth, it can be treacherous to love someone who intentionally offends you. I myself find it quite difficult to love in severe situations. God wants us all to love each other equally, but in a lot of cases we don't. One of the reasons we don't is because most of us have never been taught the difference between unconditional Agape love and emotional love. Agape love is to be acted out. Telling someone you love him or her and showing affection are ways of expressing emotional love. However, the power in agape love is displayed when you sacrifice. Giving up your needs and wants for someone who has a need is a true act of agape love. Treating a person with respect and maintaining patience, whether they disserve it or not displays love. In a monogamous relationship or marriage, you must be realistic with your expectations. Know and understand that there will be times that you will not agree. There will even be times that both of you will misunderstand and be misunderstood. While this is true, you are still obligated by Agape love to treat them with respect, remain humble, and remain patient. A lot of times we don't do that. We get upset and say things we don't mean and hurt the person's feelings. When that happens, the best way to overcome that situation is to apologize and forgive. When you do this you are sacrificing how you feel for the benefit of making that person happy. This is how some marriages have lasted so long. You have to decide what its worth to you to have a successful relationship. This goes for both men and women. It's always rewarding to forgive. It shows maturity and shows that it's not all about you. It is never ok to play 'two can play that game'. When you do this you are preserving your feelings and self-image. This is something that society teaches us to do. Be all about self. There is a difference between self-love and self-preservation. There is a fine line between them. Having love for yourself means you have self-respect. You will not let anyone mistreat you for any reason. You have to discern the difference between someone being imperfect and someone that's out to hurt you.

One main thing that every woman needs is compassion. Instead of being demanding and commanding, treat her with compassion, acknowledging her sensitivity as a woman, the weaker vessel. You are not her sergeant; you are her strong leader that leads by example of love and compassion. When she needs to come to you about a situation, she doesn't want to feel like she's going to be reprimanded like a child. She needs you to listen to her and give her corresponding feedback. A lot of times as men it's difficult for us to do this because we are decision makers. We think logically, so we may already have the answer and prefer to blurt it out to get through with the conversation. Women, on the other hand, most of the time are emotional thinkers and rationalize everything. In order to please her and keep peace, brothers, listen to your woman. This gives her the security she needs to trust you with her feelings and even her life. Deal with her according to wisdom. You cannot have the mindset that you only want to have your way. That's not love. Love says I am considering what your needs and desires are and I will do my very best at meeting them. You have to be as selfless as possible. Selfishness is the root cause of every divorce. It has been proven that if a man is proactive in meeting the needs and desires of his woman, she will do the same for him ten times over. Whatever he does for her, she gives it back to him, magnified.

Who are you?

Women love to see a good looking man who knows how to dress and smells good! But as fine as she thinks he is, who is he? This is not just for women. Most people spend more time maintaining their body and outer appearance than they do building their character. I'm a stickler for cleanliness and looking your best, but if you are relaxed about developing into being the fullness of who God purposed you to be, then the outer appearance means very little. No one will ever become perfect in the human body on this earth, but you can develop into a great person of character, loving people with no motive, loving the unlovable. You can be the most handsome and stylistic person that exists. If you are hurt, damaged, bitter, angry, confused, and except that it's ok to allow a woman to physically, verbally, and mentally abuse, focusing mostly on your outer appearance will only hinder you from overcoming those issues. You are only an asset to someone when you have inner quality as well as outer attraction to bring to the table. When you enter a relationship with deep issues and long-developed bad character you better believe it will be stressful for the both of you! It's everyone's responsibility to treat the other person right. Every person was created to help the other. How can you help someone if you haven't conquered anything? You have to be assertive in developing into greatness so that you can help someone, even the person you are dating.

If you are whole and ready to be in a relationship and you are involved with someone who is damaged, hurt, bitter, and/or struggling with acceptance/low self esteem, you don't necessarily have to run from them. If you know yourself that you have the capacity and patience to deal with them, you may just be the right person to influence deliverance and change. However, if you have done all you can to impart into that person and you've invested what you feel is precious time to influence change and, no matter how much they SAY they want to change, they show you that they want to remain in mediocrity, you can choose to get out of that situation because they're not an asset to your life and may never be. I do not find it wise to waste time with someone who can only take from you and never add anything to you. Our days on earth are anonymously numbered. There's no sense in misusing them.

Chapter 5

Stepping Up To The Plate

Money Answers All Things

For a very long time I had in my mind that when a woman wants a man with money she was a gold digger. In some cases this is true. If a woman says a man has to be making an enormous amount of money, then she is a gold digger. On the contrary, if she states that he has to have a decent paying job that allows him to take care of himself, help hold down the household bills, and do some nice things for her sometimes, that's a realistic preference. There are even women out there that are able to deal with a man that's making very little, but she is a needle in a haystack. Keep her! She loves him deeply! Even something as simple as going to the movies could be a problem for a man that is struggling to take care of himself. I know from experience. I have been in a few relationships when I was struggling to take care of myself. That was a nightmare! Lack of money was the constant argument. Maybe when you are 19 and 20 years old you can get away with dating someone while you're broke. By age 27 you're starting to date women instead of girls. For most women when they are ready to settle down, they are no longer satisfied with a simple movie and a walk in the park. They have now graduated to more expensive tastes, such as five star restaurants and expensive resorts. Long gone are the days of renting movies almost every weekend. That will be something she will appreciate doing every once in a while. Money is not all it takes to have a peaceful and successful relationship, but it makes things run a lot smoother than it would be without it. It doesn't take a millionaire to make a humble and mature woman happy. But it does take some decent cash flow and a little creativity.

The Significance Of Knowing Your Purpose

Having a job is wonderful thing. It allows you to take care of your needs and the needs of your family. However, going to work from day to day never finding your purpose is settling for mediocrity. Sisters not only want a man with a stable job, they also want a man that knows his purpose and has a vision and a plan to carry it out. Long gone are the days of settling for just getting by. I'm not saying that you have to a millionaire. But I am saying you should want to be the best at whatever it is you love to do.

It's very important to discover the purpose of your existence. How do you find your purpose? The thing you find yourself doing that gives you that unexplainable joy, and you do it without thinking about getting paid for it, that is your passion. Your passion is the very thing that God will use to help other people. It is your purpose. The next step is having a vision. Having a vision and a plan are two of the main keys to success. A vision is the specific thing that you have a desire to focus on. But without a plan to carry out that vision, it is just an idea. You have to come up with a strategic plan to carry out that fantastic vision. It may not happen overnight, but in due season it will all come together and you'll be amazed at the beauty of the empire that you have nurtured and taken your time to build. Patience and hard work is the bridge between your vision and success. To whom much is given much is required.

Having positive people around you is extremely vital for getting you to your destiny. You have to be around people who believe in you and what you are doing. I have to be honest, there will be times that you will want to give up on your dream because things may not happen when and how you want it to. Having negative energy around during those times can discourage you, making you give up on your dream. Stay away from dream killers. If you have a dream or dreams and you've given up on them, no matter how old or young you are, go ahead and get back on track and pursue them relentlessly with inevitable tenacity.

The Sum Of It All

If you really desire to meet that great woman of your dreams and settle down, take some time to evaluate or reevaluate yourself. Be 100% honest. If there is anything that you are dealing with from your past, be it childhood tragedies and inadequacies, tumultuous relationships that left painful scars, or even the disappointment from not finding love, it is to your benefit and the benefit of anyone else you date that you deal these things and began your healing process. God is just one conversation away. Spill everything out to him that is holding you prisoner to misery. Spend time with Him reading His Word to build up your spirit and your faith in Him. He is the supplier of adequacy and strength. We are human and we are forever growing, so it's not realistic to become perfect until that great day we meet Jesus. However, you must realize that you have areas where you can improve and start the improvement process. Take it day by day, thereby molding yourself into the best man that God created you to be. With His help you can reach your destiny!

PART II

To My Sisters

Chapter 6

Young, Black, & Educated

It's a wonderful accomplishment to earn your college degree. Whether you are satisfied with a bachelors degree, or aimed higher for your masters or even a PhD, the benefits can be lucratively rewarding. After all, you've worked hard and sacrificed a lot of sleep to get it. Now that you've earned it, it seems every guy you meet doesn't have his and has every excuse in the book why he can't get it. You figure if you could put all of your blood, sweat, and tears into getting yours, so can they. You've even danced right into your dream career, making your dream salary. You are able to pay all of your bills on time, some months in advance, and you're able to shop as much as you'd like. You even go on two vacations a year. Life for you is like heaven!

As great as your life is, you long for that good smelling man to hold you securely in his arms after a nice dinner and a movie. You've gone out on a few dates, but the guys you've gone out with didn't make enough money and didn't have college degrees. They were really nice guys, but you couldn't get past the fact that they didn't have as much to offer as you do.

Let me help you out here. Though getting a college degree is a great thing, it doesn't define a man's character as a man. Some actually have valid reasons for not yet earning their degree. If you meet a great man of character that doesn't have his degree but he is pursuing his dreams and passions, you shouldn't reject him. Pay close attention to him. If you see he's tenacious and walks in integrity, you can trust that he will successfully fulfill his dreams. He may not have put time into getting a degree, but he is putting time into relentlessly accomplishing his goal of doing what he loves to do.

Who are you?

I love to see a good looking woman who knows how to dress and smells good! Not only can she dress, she knows how to bargain shop, looking like a million dollars! There's one question I have in mind every time I lay eyes on woman of this caliber . . . . who is she? Most people spend more time maintaining their body and outer appearance than they do building their character. I'm a stickler for cleanliness and looking your best, but if you are relaxed about developing into the fullness of who God purposed you to be, then the outer appearance means very little. No one will ever become perfect in the human body on this earth, but you can develop into a great person of character, loving people with no motive, loving the unlovable. You can be the most beautiful and stylistic person that exists. If you are hurt, damaged, bitter, angry, confused, and except that it's ok to allow a man to physically, verbally, and mentally abuse you, focusing mostly on your outer appearance will only hinder you from overcoming those issues. You are only an asset to someone when you have inner quality as well as outer attraction to bring to the table. When you enter a relationship with deep issues and long-developed bad character you better believe it will be stressful for the both of you! It's everyone's responsibility to treat the other person right. Every person was created to help the other. How can you help someone if you haven't conquered anything, and you're void of substance? You have to be assertive in developing into greatness so that you will be an asset to their life and a strong stable bridge to their future. If you are whole and ready to be in a relationship and you are involved with someone who is damaged, hurt, bitter, and/or struggling with acceptance/low self esteem, you don't necessarily have to run from them. If you know yourself that you have the capacity and patience to deal with them, you may just be the right person to influence deliverance and change. However, if you have done all you can to impart into that person and you've invested what you feel is precious time to influence change and, no matter how much they SAY they want to change, they show you that they want to remain in mediocrity, you can choose to get out of that situation because they're not an asset to your life and may never be. I do not find it wise to waste time with someone who can only take from you and never add anything to you. Our days on earth are anonymously numbered. There's no sense in misusing them.

Being His Partner On The Path Of Purpose

When a man and a woman get together they are partners. Initially, it starts as mere friendship. During the friendship stage, just as it is with being friends with someone of the same sex, you help each other in time of need. A lot of women forget that this man is your friend. It's fine for him to help her financially, but when he is in need of help she thinks it's inappropriate to help him. If you are friends, why does the gender matter? Both male and female should be able to build a great friendship without putting demands on each other according to gender. When making the decision to be in an intimate monogamous relationship with each other, be sure to communicate what you expect from each other. This will eliminate unnecessary frustration and arguments. If you decide to be with a man that has yet to establish himself, make sure that you can handle being there for him even while he is still building his empire. I admit it does take a lot of patience, longsuffering, and perseverance to faithfully be there for him, but that's what love does. Most men would rather have a woman right by there side as they are climbing the road to success. But there are others are more comfortable waiting until they have reached a certain level of success before they feel they are ready to settle down. It is, however, a beautiful thing for a man to be able to say that his jewel was there at the beginning, going through the highs and lows with him, and still there when everything has all come together. You will be able to look back and say that you built a spectacular empire together. This automatically builds an unbreakable bond. Always keep in mind that two heads are better than one.

Chapter 7

Playing The Game

If there is one thing that I have learned, is that a woman has the ability to make a man weak and do whatever she wants him to do. She knows and understands very well that every man's weakness is a woman. A woman can go years with out dating a man, but a man can hardly go one month without dating a woman. Being that men are 90% visual, a woman knows that all she has to do is put on the right outfit and work the right hair style and she can get a man's attention. It could be something as simple as a pair of jeans from Wal-Mart. She knows what jeans compliment her curves. While she's looking debonair, she's got the right conversation and the confidence to go with it. If she's really on her A game, she can make the most successful 'Player' fall for her. The strategies of the game are all the same with men and women, but a woman holds much more power than a man. It has been that way since Adam and Eve.

Though all this playing may seem quite fun, it can result to something catastrophic. Within the last few years there have been several cases of men murdering their wives and girlfriends, and even their own children. You have to be careful about whom you choose to deal with and how you choose to deal with them. Just as a woman finds out that her man is cheating and she lashes out on him, a man is capable of doing the same thing. As I mentioned to the men in the first segment of this book, dating is for getting to know yourself as you get to know people. It's not to use people or to see how many people you can humiliate. It's fine to date more than one person at a time, letting each person know that you are dating and you are not yet ready for commitment. I am in know way condoning domestic violence, but I am saying that it is a reality that if a person learns that they have been deceived, they may do something that you will both regret. You may think you know a person, and you may think that you have all of your T's crossed and all of your I's dotted. You have to understand that any of us in the right situation are capable of doing something that we will later regret. As the old saying goes, treat people the way you want to be treated. No one wants to be played and deceived. That may be an old saying, but it is the true way of keeping peace in your life and having peace with everyone that you come into contact with. If you have friends that are playing the game, it may be a great idea to get away from that negative atmosphere. Your environment shapes your way of thinking.

Chapter 8

The Anatomy Of A Man

What makes a man? God created man to be a leader and the initiator. A man has the most important role in a family. Everyone is depending upon him for the security and provision that they need. There is a clear distinction between a man and a woman. There are things that a man was created to do that a woman was not created to do, and vise versa. Because a man is the leader, his role in the family consists of making sure his family has a safe and pleasant living environment, making sure the mechanics of the home are well maintained, keeping the grass cut, taking out the trash, and if there are children in the home, he makes sure he gives them the love and support that that they need, leading by example. According to their agreement, a man and a woman can share the responsibility in some of those things I just mentioned. However, a woman has her own significant role. She was created to help and nurture. She gives compliment to the man by partnering with him only to help him.

Many marriages result in divorce because the man is not completely walking in his role as the leader. The wife feels she has to lead, and the results are not pretty. Instead of her being the helper, she's the helper and the leader. This is out of order. I'm making this point to paint a picture of what things are and what they should be. There are some men out there that are good at taking care of home, as far as maintaining a great job and paying bills on time. Some of those same men are not being faithful to their wives. A lot of times men cheat just out of greed. Other times he feels that his woman is not complimenting him the way that she should.

His Needs

No matter what the situation is, there is never a reason to be unfaithful. However, it happens everyday. The number one need of every man is respect. If his woman is not respecting him, he finds that as a reason to cheat. This is one of the main reasons why men cheat. When coming home from a hard days work, he wants to come home to a peaceful and clean environment. If both spouses work, it's a great idea to discuss and come to an agreement on sharing responsibilities in the home. When talking to him, just as a woman doesn't want to be talked to in a condescending tone of voice, he wants to be treated with love and compassion, honoring his leadership. If all she does is nag and complain, that makes him feel as though she doesn't appreciate the man that he is, which pushes him away. If he's not fully walking in his role as the head, instead of mistreating him, communicate to him what your needs are and what it's going to take to run your household in harmony. You can guarantee better results when you are proactive as apposed to being reactive. Show him that you appreciate his strengths, while compassionately communicating to him that you recognize his weaknesses and you are willing to help him become a better man. Not one of us walking this earth is perfect. Love says I will be patient with you, walking with a meek and humble attitude. I'm sure you want that same love and respect.

The second thing I would like to point out as one the basic needs of a man is his need to be sexually satisfied. This of course is within the covenant of a marriage. First of all ladies, I'm sure you know that men are 90% visual. What we see triggers what we feel. Women, on the other hand, are turned on by what you say to them and how you say it, and what you do and how you do it. An older gentleman once told me that you don't start making love to your wife in the bedroom. It starts from the time you get up that morning. How a man treats his woman throughout the day determines her sexual desire for him. With all that being said, men can desire to have sex anytime and anywhere. It's like an essential vitamin that we need! Seriously, some women have very high sex drives, but most men between the ages of 18-40 have extremely high sex drives. With this being said, as a woman you have to understand a man's sexual needs and make sure you're open to communicate with him his specific sexual needs. I would even say that, during the dating stages, it's a great idea to discuss this so that you don't go into marriage not knowing each other's specific sexual desires. This way, you will know what to expect and neither of you can say that you didn't know.

As I make my final point on this particular matter, I would like to reiterate that a man is a leader. However, God apparently felt that he needed a helper. This helper, that He so graciously named woman, was created as the weaker part of him. Not that she's weaker mentally or even physically, but weaker in the sense of her being the person that helps a man do what he was already doing. Her role is not to initiate his plan or road to his destiny. She was created to aide him, giving him the support that is similar to that of a mother. A mother is there to validate you and build your confidence. In like, a woman compliments the confidence he already has. She is his confidant. I have seen so many women degrade and belittle the man they are involved with when he's faced with adversity, trying to destroy him. As I said earlier, a man is the leader, so he should be able to control his emotions. Subsequently, there are going to be moments that he is faced with challenges, and he may need his woman's love and compassion. That is how you help him as oppose to tearing him down.

Granting His Wishes

We all have our individual needs and desires. It's important that we communicate to each other what those things are. There are three main causes for divorce: infidelity, lack of finances, and lack of communication. All of these are results of the lack of communication. Both the man and the woman should be mature enough to communicate to each other what their needs and wants are. As I said earlier, this is a part of the dating stage. If you wait until you're married to talk about your desires, you may be surprised at what you here and may even disagree with granting those particular wishes. You may even have a lack of confidence in fulfilling the requests. This is a part of getting to know each other. By the time you're married, you will both be up on what it takes to please each other. As his wife, it is your responsibility to grant his wishes, as you see fit morally, just as it is his responsibility to meet yours. Some things may come out that he didn't mention before you got married. Handle that maturely and try to come to an agreement. It's my heart's desire to see people get married and maintain a healthy marriage. You cannot get married with the mindset of only getting your needs and desires met. It will not work. You have to be as selfless as possible. That's what love is. Always consider your man's needs and desires and do your very best at meeting them.

Chapter 9

What Is Your Motive?

Many people get married for various reasons. Some people get married because they are in love and want to share the rest of their lives with that person, knowing there is no real unconditional love there for that person. Some people get married for financial security, financial greed, if children are involved, they marry so that both parents will raise the children, or for the sake of being alone For women, the wedding day is the most important day of their lives.

A lot of them get married just for that day. Thousands and even sometimes millions of dollars are spent on weddings for couples that only stay married for two years. In today's time, very few people get married out of pure love. Some people get married because of their religious beliefs.

I have to be vivid and honest here. If you are not marrying a person out of pure unconditional love and wanting to give your entire life to this person for the rest of your life, you are marrying for the wrong reason. It's fine to be in love. There should be plenty of passion. But if you don't love this person unconditionally, your marriage will end in divorce court. I'm not implying that anyone is perfect, but I am saying that life is what you make it. Life itself comes with challenges that we all have to be strong enough to overcome. There's no sense in adding drama that can be avoided. Life is about making mistakes and learning from them. I'm not condemning anyone who did marry for the wrong reason. If you've already ended that marriage, it's to your benefit, and your children's benefit, if you have any, that you make a wise choice as to who you will spend the rest of your life with. Though we are imperfect people, we are all capable of doing our best at making the best choices for our future.

For The Love Of Money

Money makes the world go 'round. Oh how true this statement is. With money one can accomplish many things. Without money, one will never advance to their fullest potential. We live according to a system we call credit. If a person sees something that they want, they can charge it to a credit card and pay either the minimum credit card payment, or if they can, pay the entire balance. Everything we do is based upon our credibility. In order for a bank to loan you money, they have to see proof that you pay all of your bills on time. This ensures them that they will get their money back, with interest, on time. If you are not financially stable, it is very difficult to pay your bills on time. This also makes it difficult to establish great credit. It's very important that a man establishes a dependable stable job or career that enables him to pay his bills on time. He will then be able to establish great credit. At the point that he feels he's ready to settle down with a woman, he will already have himself together, which makes things run smooth when he takes on the responsibility of taking her to be his wife. This is his role as the leader.

A woman also wants to have some freedom to be able to buy nice things, whether she buys it or he buys it. If she buys something, she wants to be able to do it knowing she can still pay all of her bills on time and save money as well. These are things that a woman should consider when choosing her mate.

If you are greedy and selfish thinking that you have to have everything that you want when you want it, this is dangerous for you and surely the wrong reason to get married. A lot of women have this motive. When they meet men, the first question they ask is what is his occupation and what is his salary. If he's doing fairly well for himself, they will marry him for his money. She may not even like him. There's absolutely no compatibility. Once she realizes that she can't take it anymore, she files for a divorce. For some, this becomes a pattern. As important as money is in any marriage, it should not be your sole or main reason for marrying someone. If you think back on a lot of people you've seen do this, they all ended up either in divorce court or committing adultery or both. Those that stayed together were miserable because they're financially set but there's no love in the marriage.

For Financial Security

A large number of people in the African-American community get married because in order to run a household, it may be cheaper for them to put both incomes together. As innocent as this may sound, this should not be the reason you marry someone. This can be one of the reasons, but not the main one. If you don't love this person and there's no true compatibility, you should not marry them. Unconditional love, respect, and compatibility have to be in place in order to have a healthy long lasting marriage.

For The Children

When kids are involved, whether you had them before you met each other, or together before marriage, it is important to make the decision that is best for them. It's vital that a child has a safe, loving, and peaceful environment. To marry someone just so that the children will have both parents in the home can be just as bad as living in a single-parent home. Once again, if there's no mutual unconditional love for each other and no compatibility, it's a waste of time for both you and the kids. It can be a nightmare. My parents are great examples of this. When my mother and father met, my mother already had two girls. She was living with my grandmother, struggling to take care of my two sisters. I guess my dad and her felt some sort of love connection. So, he married her to help her take care of the girls. Then a few months later I was conceived. I can remember growing up as a kid my mom and dad would argue all the time. I could see that there was some kind of love there, but no compatibility. By the time I was nine years old they had decided to end the marriage.

This is the case with so many of us. We have to make wiser decisions when we are considering the person we will spend the rest of our lives with. I was blessed that the chaos that took place in our home didn't affect me. However, not many people come out as gracefully as I did. Things such as verbal and physical abuse, molestation, rape, and neglect are unfortunate catastrophes that happen in homes where there is no love with mentally unstable individuals. These things usually have a major affect on children. For many it takes years to overcome situations of this magnitude. Divorce itself can damage a child. It can result in a child misbehaving in school, lashing out, and can even cause them to not want to get close to someone, in fear that the person will leave them. Your child should be your main priority. When you think you are in love with someone, be sure that this person is a great fit for you and your children. I had a friend who chose to satisfy her own desire of being with a man, not considering her daughter at all. She would always say that because her daughter was an adolescent, she was smart enough to understand that her mother has needs. She said that she was not going to be and old maid. A few months down the road the guy she was seeing started abusing her. Last I heard she was still with him. You can't be concerned only for yourself. Your children should be your primary concern. An abusive man will not only abuse you, but he will also abuse your children. Your child may seem ok with your decision, but soon you will see how much it affects them. They may end up making the same type of choices you made, and now it's a vicious cycle. As parents, you are the living example of life. What your children see you do, they will do some of the same things. You may think you'll be fine with it now, but when it actually happens you will regret it.

A child needs a well balanced and stable home. Having several men around shows instability and the child will began to lose trust in you. If you have a daughter, it is especially important to live a lifestyle that shows dignity and respect for yourself. If you don't respect yourself, she won't respect you neither will she respect herself. To avoid causing your child/children unnecessary hurt and pain, please be wise in choosing your mate.

The Antidote For Loneliness

We were all put here to fulfill the purposes that God has planned for us. For those that desire it, this plan includes a mate. In my opinion, no one wants to be alone. Some people may be fine with just having pets or spending time with family. I believe that we can all agree that every human being that exists on earth wants to have companionship. With this being established, many of us hurry to get married because we don't want to be alone. Some for spiritual reasons believe that it's the right thing to do. Some even marry to escape the temptation of pre-marital sex. Being that marriage is sacred and meant to last forever, you can't just marry someone because they fill that void of emptiness. In most cases, if not in all, when a person marries because they just had to have the companionship, they end up divorced. A lot of times a child is born during the marriage. Sadly, this results in raising the child from two separate homes, which can be difficult. I believe it is safe to say that even when you are in the dating stages you shouldn't do it out of desperation.

Ladies, I know that this can be difficult for you. I understand that you are emotional and you long for a man to be there to hold you at night. Just the thought of having him there to listen to you and make you feel special and wine and dine you makes you quiver. He's your protection from any harm.

In order to be ready for your mate, you have to be confident in who you are and understand that you don't have to be with someone to feel validated. A lot of times women feel validated when a man is there to compliment her and take care of her. Validation comes from your parents, family, and friends. If you didn't get that validation, you have to validate yourself. Even if you did get it from them, you still have to believe in yourself, being confident in who you are. You may ask, "How do I validate myself?" This is done by spending time alone, learning your likes and dislikes, discovering your strengths and weaknesses, embracing everything good about you, and discovering your passions. In doing this, you begin to love who you are. Even though you have imperfections, you appreciate and embrace your strengths and your passions. If you see any sign of insecurity, search yourself to see what you feel you are uncomfortable with. You are human. We all have something that we don't like that we can change. Don't be afraid to confront those insecurities and deal with them so that you can overcome them. Maybe it's something physical that you can't change. Use that as a mark of uniqueness and embrace everything that defines you as the beautiful woman that God created you to be. This is also called self-development. The desire to be with a man will still be there, but only to just simply love and be loved. You will have control over your emotions and you'll be able to clearly make a decision as to whom you will entertain. I do believe that having great friends that you can count on is very vital for self-development. It's healthy to go out and have fun, experiencing different things and exposing yourself to various positive environments. It's also great to have friends that will give you positive criticism. This helps you to build great character and strengthen yourself in areas where you have room for improvement.

Marriage is a very serious and sacred covenant. It's not to be taken as a license to control and have your way, neither should it be taken as a sex license. Its' purpose is to have that partner there that you can trust to share your life with; your ups, your downs, your successes and your failures.

What Lies Beneath

The greatest responsibility of mankind is to treat people the way we want to be treated, loving them as we love ourselves. To love and just simply do right by people is the absolute most powerful influential thing, yet is the hardest thing for most people to do. To be loved or not beloved determines our present and our future. From birth, every baby boy and every baby girl's life depends on attention, affection, and must be nurtured. If any of these things are omitted, more than likely the child will suffer from rejection. It is love that keeps us fresh, colorful, energetic, aware, and last but not least, confident. As I stated earlier, when a father is not present in the life of a child, girl or boy, therein is the absence leadership, affirmation and discipline. Girls have an innate yearning for male affirmation, attention, and validation. As she goes on from day to day without her father, know matter how pretty she is, no matter how many people tell her she is pretty, no matter how many boys show her some attention, which gets vulgar as they grow older, she will always feel a massive void. In turn, she does various things to gain attention from boys, and even if the attention is grotesquely degrading she will accept it. As she begins to physically develop, she takes notice of it and likes the reaction she gets from the young boys. Her soft gentle heart falls for one of them, thinking of him every minute of the day, sun up to sun down. He one day tries to deprive her of her innocence. She doesn't want to because she has no clue what sex about and she's afraid. He tells her the famous words, "I love you and if you love me you will do it", or "if you don't do it I will break up with you." Afraid that he will leave her or go out with another girl, she does it. Afterwards she feels dirty, confused, and thinks less of herself. If those feelings weren't treacherous enough, the next day in school he walks by her as if he doesn't know her. She approaches him only to have her heart shattered by the words, "Get away from me." This situation can create one or two outcomes. She will either continue to search for love, attention, affection, and affirmation from guys, and if she doesn't deal with her issues she will continue this pattern into adulthood, or she will become bitter, cold hearted, and afraid to love, afraid to give her heart, putting up a wall/guard of defense, and possibly treat men the way she has been treated. In a lot of cases young women began to feel that they can gain love from a guy by giving him her body. If she never cries out to God for the love and validation she lacked from her father, she will grow older in age but never in her mind. She may progress and thrive in her career and indulge in material things, but because she never received love her soul never fully developed. There are other things that contribute to low self worth, (i.e. rape, molestation physical, verbal, and emotional abuse) If you have experienced the horrible misfortune of these gruesome catastrophes, our loving, warm, and compassionate God is here to love you profusely, eager to take away the pain from the years upon years of violation, loneliness, anger, bitterness, and emptiness. He will fill that void with love that is electrifying, life giving, purpose giving, and the feeling of completion. You no longer have to be a product of your catastrophe! Underneath all of the grime, the guilt, shame, and pain, you were made in the image of God. Therefore, you are beautiful, you are valid, He has given you purpose, you have more worth than anyone could ever give you because God gave it to you! The truth of the matter is, hurt people hurt people. When you enter into a relationship or marriage broken and damaged, it's not that the relationship can't work, but the things that will come out of you could damage the person you are with. Relationships already require a lot of work, with daily sacrifices for the happiness and peace of your mate. Peace in your home doesn't come by continuous friction. It is better to have a stable, healed and peaceful heart and mind than to be bottled up with unanswered questions and unhealed wounds from your past. Everyone has something that they have experienced that effected them in a negative way. We have to make an executive decision that we are greater than our tragedies. It is from our tragedies that we are made strong. No great body builder gained maximum strength and massive muscular structure by lifting the same weight size he began with. It was the education of health and exercising with consistent dedication to do it as part of their lifestyle. Consciously read your bible daily for comfort, empowerment, and instruction, and put into action what you read, one day at a time. All that you need to break free and truly enjoy abundant life is there. God's ways are the best ways to walk in peace and wholeness. Change your life, change your family legacy!

> I pray the day will come that you adhesively connect with the man of God who will appreciate, embrace and protect your worth! YOUR WORTH IS PRICELESS!

Being Realistic About Mr. Right

Considering all the topics we have discussed, you now have to ask yourself are you being realistic about the mate of your destiny. There are many factors that play a part into choosing that special someone. Just as you are not perfect, the mate of your destiny will not be perfect either. We are forever growing and our interests change as we develop. What you like at 25 you may no longer have that same interest at 35. What you were undeveloped in at 25 you may have flourished into by 35. You have to look at men the same way. Just because he's the head doesn't mean he will be free from idiosyncrasies. Some things he will grow out of and into, some things he won't. You have to put things in their proper perspective. For some finances may be more important, for another communication and affection, and for another communication and compatibility. I will give you twelve things to consider when choosing the mate of your destiny should be these:

1. Does he have a solid relationship with God? 2.
2. Does he treat you with respect and love you unconditionally, loving and accepting you for who you are?
3. How developed is his character?
4. If he has children, is he taking care of them and active in their lives?
5. Does he communicate effectively with you?
6. Is he honest and trustworthy?
7. Do you share some of the same interests and views, which makes you compatible?
8. Can the two of you agree to disagree with each other instead of debating and brawling?
9. Is he mentally and emotionally stable?
10. Does he have a job?
11. Does he know his purpose, have a vision, a plan, and ambition to pursue it?
12. Is he responsible at handling his business?

If these things are in place, you have a great man. I learned the hard way that if you are superficial, you'll end up alone. You don't have to be alone when you meet someone that has all of the qualities I just mentioned. You may have already met a man that has these qualities and your regretting that you passed him up. Don't be discouraged. Life is about learning from the bad choices that you make. Don't condemn yourself. If you're paying attention, in due season, you will meet another great man of valor. This time you will appreciate and embrace him. Marriage is not about vanity and temporary gratification; it's about life-long commitment to love and to serve. There may be times of discomfort and inconvenience, but it is an honor to give someone the advantage instead of taking advantage.

Chapter 10

Final Point: Love:
What Is It?

What is this thing we call love? Some say it's a feeling. Some say it's a knowing in your soul. Some say it's about sacrifice. Some say it's a thing worth dying for. To others it's just a word used to express emotions. The expression I hear most often is it's unconditional.

We often hear people say they are in love, but the minute that person they're in love with does something that disappoints them, they are ready to give up and leave. The term 'in love' is an expression of ones' emotional state at its' highest level. This type of love in its' Greek meaning is *eros, of* which the term erotica is derived from. It is described as passionate love with sensual desire and longing. You can be in love with someone and not love them unconditionally. You can simply be turned on emotionally by something they are doing to you or for you that gives that overwhelming emotional feeling, or just simply adore them for the very person that they are. Just as easily, that same person can do something you view as being inappropriate and those emotions will dissipate, causing you to feel emotionally down. Maybe even upset to the point of anger. Ironically that emotional high can flare up or melt down a million times over.

Unconditional love in its' greek meaning is *agapeo* or *agape*. When you love someone with gape love, they haven't done anything to earn it. You can be in love at first sight and/or with more than one person at a time, but you can only be faithfully and intimately committed to one of them, which is monogamy. You may be asking, "How can I love and be in love with more than one person at a time?" As I previously stated, being in love is just an emotional high. Several people at a time can make you feel this way. Agape love, however, is an inevitable trait from God that we all inherited from Him. We just have to operate in it! For most of us, we operate in that love when it is most convenient for us. In truth, it can be treacherous to love someone who intentionally offends you. I myself find it quite difficult to love in severe situations. God wants us all to love each other equally, but in a lot of cases we don't. One of the reasons we don't is because most of us have never been taught the difference between unconditional Agape love and emotional love. Agape love is to be acted out. Telling someone you love him or her and showing affection are ways of expressing emotional love. However, the power in agape love is displayed when you sacrifice. Giving up your needs and wants for someone who has a need is a true act of agape love. Treating a person with respect and maintaining patience, whether they disserve it or not displays love. In a monogamous relationship or marriage, you must be realistic with your expectations. Know and understand that there will be times that you will not agree. There will even be times that both of you will misunderstand and be misunderstood. While this is true, you are still obligated by Agape love to treat them with respect, remain humble, and remain patient. A lot of times we don't do that. We get upset and say things we don't mean and hurt the person's feelings. When that happens, the best way to overcome that situation is to apologize and forgive. When you do this you are sacrificing how you feel for the benefit of making that person happy. This is how some marriages have lasted so long. You have to decide what its worth to you to have a successful relationship. This goes for both men and women. It's always rewarding to forgive. It shows maturity and shows that it's not all about you.

It is never ok to play 'two can play that game'. When you do this you are preserving your feelings and self-image. This is something that society teaches us to do. Be all about self. There is a difference between self-love and self-preservation. There is a fine line between them. Having love for yourself means you have self-respect. You will not let anyone mistreat you for any reason. You have to discern the difference between someone being imperfect and someone that's out to hurt you. As humans, we don't have any intentions on telling someone we love them until we feel it and until we feel the time is right. Love is not a feeling. Imagine buying a puppy. After a few days, you can easily become emotionally attached to it. If something happens to it, you may get emotional and cry. If the puppy has been around for a long time, it could take you a while to get over the loss. Emotional love gives a warm feeling and sparks energy and motivation, but agape love is the only thing that will sustain you through the tests of time. If you are not developed in agape love before you yoke up with someone, it could hinder you from having a successful relationship. You can, however make great use of the opportunity to develop in love while dating that person. No one is perfect. We are all humans depending on God to make us the best humans we can be. All we have to do is depend on Him. When going into a marriage, you must be developed in love and have the character development to maintain an everlasting successful marriage.

Taking The Love Class

How do you learn how to love with agape love? God is the greatest teacher. He is the creator of love. If you don't have a relationship with God, it will be very difficult to understand what love is and how to express it. I whole-heartedly encourage you to give Him a chance to show you just how much He loves you and how to share it with others. No one can love God without first loving yourself, realizing that you need Him and reaching out to Him. A person can say they love God, but if they haven't developed love for themselves, how can you love someone else, even God himself. It is only at that moment of realizing that you DO have worth and you need God for growth and guidance that you not only cling to God, but show Him how much value He has in your life. In order for one to love, that love has to already be in your heart for self, outpouring to another. The first person who should receive that love is God. How do you show God you love Him? Just like a male/female relationship, the more time you spend with God, the more the love for Him grows. The more your love for Him grows, the more you see yourself in

His image, realizing and maximizing your self worth. You also show God you love Him by obeying His word and divine instruction. Even as you do this, the most significant way to show God you love Him is by loving others. Not solely with the emotional love, but foremost with the never failing ever winning agape unconditional love. The love that respects, considers, and ultimately serves. God has a magnificent plan for each and every one of us. We have the freedom to make the choice to allow Him to get in the driver's seat and help us fulfill it.

Accepting Christ as your savior is the first step to establishing a relationship with God. Every need and desire you have God will provide it to you. All of the guidelines for life are in His word. Growing and developing a great Godly lifestyle consists of so many things. I like to think of it as a box with many parts to assemble one whole product. Each part is essential for molding a great man or woman into a masterpiece. If you want to know how to prepare for the mate of your destiny, this is the way. When you spend time submitting to God, you will be ready to submit to your mate. As you grow spiritually, you encounter so many different experiences that build character and patience. You will always have obstacles when you're with someone because you are both human and you each have your own identity. This requires a lot of patience and character, which is love. People are killing their families because they have no confidence in who they are. There is no definition to their lives. No conviction. God is the one who defines you. In order to have real confidence in yourself you have to have great confidence in God. You have to walk by faith, trusting Him that He will take care of everything that concerns you. Just take a few moments to reflect on a time you didn't know how you were going to make it through a situation.

Right when you thought all was going to crumble, God stepped in and everything worked out. I'm sure you can think of several times that this has happened. Have you ever needed something to come through immediately and it did? That was God. Every time you are faced with trials, remember all the ones God brought you through. This is how you build your confidence in Him. You are human and very much subject to error. It's your confidence in God that will get you through things that you couldn't dare get out of without Him, His peace, and is His love. His provision is His love. His comfort is His love. His word is His love.

What do you have to lose besides your soul? I truly believe we all believe in God. It didn't surprise me that when the tragedy happened on Sept. 11 2001 the churches were filled. It was no big surprise that when Hurricane Katrina hit the churches were packed with people who wanted comfort from God. Let's not wait until something catastrophic happens to run to God. Run to Him because you know you love Him and you need Him everyday and every moment of your life. It's so comforting to know that God is with you no matter where you are. It's so refreshing to know that He is providing for you, from the biggest thing to the smallest. He is well worth your life.

I hope that you will meditate on the things I have covered in this book. As you meditate on each subject, take a look at your life and see if any of these things relate to you. If so, my prayer is that you make the necessary changes for the benefit of living a long peaceful and prosperous life. I leave you with words that I live by everyday of my life; to whom much is given, much is required.

Thank You's

First and foremost I thank God for creating me. I'm more than honored to be His son, servant, His vessel, and His voice to love and help my brothers and sisters. God I love you beyond emotions. I will continue to be available to you. I thank my mother Mary P. Warren for allowing me to be hard headed to experience all that was necessary for growth so that I could help set my people free from bondage! I thank my phenomenally precious baby girl Faith Victorya!! If you only knew how much you mean to me and the strength you add to me daily!!! You inspire and empower daddy to press beyond pressing, THANK YOU FOR BEING MY SWEET LITTLE SNUGGLE!!!! I thank my beautiful jewel Carla Wallace for being the Proverbs 31 that God knows I need! I appreciate you so dearly for all that you have sacrificed to see me flourish in the fullness of what God has purposed me to be! You will be GREATLY REWARDED! I thank my two sisters Melody Pender and Kontina Pippen for keeping me in line and balanced! I love you much! I thank my two closest and ABSOLUTE GREATEST friends Nick Johnson and Brandon Beasley! Man ole man ole man have we been through the wilderness, the Red Sea, the, and hell on earth!!! You guys fought this thing called life out with me when I REALLY thought I couldn't make it!!! Love you bruhs!!!! I thank my boy Arnold Smith for making me laugh at my lowest moments! Let's get these songs on the top of the charts with bullets!! Thank you LaRita Parker, Alecia "Frances" Dixon, Veronica Paschall-Buckins and all of my intelligent sisters from another mother for your valuable advise, insight, and words of encouragement, no matter how crazy my situation was!!! You helped me understand what the needs and values of a woman. I can now truly say I am ready to help heal the souls of my lovely sisters and share my life with my Proverbs 31!!! A special thanks to my pastor Dr. Luke Hall and my New Vision Christian Church Family for feeding me my daily nutrients, preparing me for my journey. Thank you Dr. Hall for your priceless humility and genuine love for your people. God will never stop rewarding you for your heart of gold! I am overjoyed and proud to be a part of your vision, a serving passenger on your road to destiny!!! I also must state that two of my biggest inspirations that have greatly influenced me as a black man coming from poverty, showing me that I CAN succeed as I pursue that which God has purposed and called me to do, no matter what obstacles I face, Mr. Steve Harvey and Mr. Tyler Perry. You two have truly shown me that I don't have to be a professional sports player, I don't have to rap, and college is great, but not the end all say all!! I am in such awe of your progression in your careers. BLACK MEN CAN!!! A HUGE thanks to my former pastor Dr. Creflo Dollar for such profound simple teaching! It was exactly what I needed to grow from a boy into a man!!!! There is a gentleman that has been the astonishing example of the truth that yes, men can love, Bishop T. D. Jakes. Your passion for the healing and success of individuals and families is something that we share, though we are miles apart. Thank you for blazing the trail for the young men to follow and mirror valor, compassion, and impeccable work and business ethic!!! If there are any others that I didn't mention, you know you have a significant place in my heart!